Prayers of Hope and Light

THOMAS KINKADE

HARVEST HOUSE™ PUBLISHERS

EUGENE, OREGON

Prayers of Hope and Light

Copyright © 2003 by Media Arts Group, Inc., Morgan Hill, CA 95037

Published by Harvest House Publishers, Eugene OR, 97402

ISBN 0-7369-0634-7

Media Arts Group, Inc.
900 Lightpost Way
Morgan Hill, CA 95037
1.800.366.3733

Design and production by Koechel Peterson & Associates, Inc., Minneapolis, Minnesota

Printed in Hong Kong

03 04 05 06 07 08 09 10 11/ NG / 10 9 8 7 6 5 4 3 2 1

Prayer is the voice
of faith directed to God.

BILLY GRAHAM

*G*OD, MAKE MY LIFE A LITTLE LIGHT,

Within the world to glow;

A little flame that burneth bright,

Wherever I may go.

God, make my life a little flower,

That giveth joy to all,

Content to bloom in native bower,

Although the place be small.

God, make my life a little song,

That comforteth the sad,

That helpeth others to be strong,

And makes the singer glad.

M. BETHAM EDWARDS

Prayer is the soul's sincere desire,
Uttered or unexpressed,
The motion of a hidden fire
That trembles in the breast.

JAMES MONTGOMERY

*J*ESUS, TENDER SHEPHERD, HEAR ME;

Bless Your little lamb tonight;

Through the darkness please be near me;

Keep me safe till morning light.

All this day Your hand has led me;

And I thank You for Your care;

You have warmed and clothed and fed me;

Listen to my evening prayer.

AUTHOR UNKNOWN

I have had prayers answered—
most strangely so sometimes—
but I think our heavenly Father's
loving-kindness has been even more
evident in what He has refused me.

LEWIS CARROLL

CALL ON YOU, O GOD, FOR YOU WILL ANSWER ME;

give ear to me and hear my prayer. Show the wonder of your great love,

you who save by your right hand those who take refuge in you from

their foes. Keep me as the apple of your eye; hide me in the shadow

of your wings...

THE BOOK OF PSALMS

*A satisfying prayer life elevates and
purifies every act of body and mind
and integrates the entire personality
into a single spiritual unit. In the long
pull, we pray only as well as we live.*

A. W. TOZER

ND THEN OUR EYES ARE OPEN WIDE

To see what we can do;

Unfold our hands so we can help,

They can be useful too;

Rise to our feet, so they will run

On errands through the day:

We like to feel that we can help,

Each in our special way.

LOUISE MARSHALL HAYNES

Prayer is not monologue but dialogue;
God's voice in response to mine is its
most essential part. Listening to God's
voice is the secret of the assurance
that He will listen to mine.

ANDREW MURRAY

Thomas
Kinkade

THE EARTH, THE SEA, THE AIR AND CLOUDS,

I know were made by Thee.

And though, dear God, You are so great,

I know You always hear me.

I put my trust in You, dear God,

I have no help but Thee;

Help my heart to keep Your laws,

Wherever I may be.

A VICTORIAN PRAYER

Prayer is action. By it we step out in advance of all other results…Praying is an activity upon which all others depend. By prayer we establish a beachhead for the kingdom among peoples where it has never been before. Prayer strikes the winning blow.

DAVID BRYANT

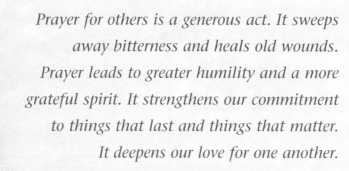

O GOD, who givest us not only the day for labor and the night for rest, but also the peace of this blessed day; grant, we beseech Thee, that its quiet may be profitable to us in heavenly things, and refresh and strengthen us to finish the work which Thou hast given us to do; through Jesus Christ our Lord. Amen.

JAMES MARTINEAU

Prayer for others is a generous act. It sweeps away bitterness and heals old wounds. Prayer leads to greater humility and a more grateful spirit. It strengthens our commitment to things that last and things that matter. It deepens our love for one another.

Prayer also deepens faith, reminding us of great truths: Evil and suffering are only for a time; love and hope endure. Even in the world's most bitter conflicts, prayer reminds us of God's love and grace, His mercy and faithfulness, the hope He provides and the peace He promises.

GEORGE W. BUSH

Thomas Kinkade

The prayer of
a righteous man
is powerful and effective.

THE BOOK OF JAMES

ETERNAL FATHER OF MY SOUL, let my first thought today be of Thee, let my first impulse be to worship Thee, let my first speech be Thy name, let my first action be to kneel before Thee in prayer.

JOHN BAILLIE

More holiness give me,

More striving within;

More patience in suffering,

More sorrow for sin;

More faith in my Savior,

More sense of His care;

More joy in His service,

More purpose in prayer.

PHILIP P. BLISS
"MY PRAYER"

*L*ORD, MAKE ME AN INSTRUMENT OF YOUR PEACE; where there is hatred, let me sow love; where there is injury, pardon; where there is doubt, faith; where there is despair, hope; where there is darkness, light; where there is sadness, joy.

O Divine Master, grant that I may not so much seek to be consoled as to console; to be understood as to understand; to be loved as to love; for it is in giving that we receive, it is in pardoning that we are pardoned, and it is in dying that we are born to eternal life.

ST. FRANCIS OF ASSISI

When the trials of this life make you weary

And your troubles seem too much to bear,

There's a wonderful solace and comfort

In the silent communion of prayer.

ANONYMOUS

Thomas Kinkade

ALMIGHTY GOD, FATHER OF ALL MERCIES, we Your unworthy servants give You humble thanks for all Your goodness and loving-kindness to us and to all men. We bless You for our creation, preservation, and all the blessings of this life; but above all for Your incomparable love in the redemption of the world by our Lord Jesus Christ; for the means of grace, and for the hope of glory. Our Father, let the spirit of gratitude so prevail in our hearts that we may manifest Thy spirit in our lives. Amen.

W. B. SLACK

The LORD detests the sacrifice of the wicked, but the prayer of the upright pleases him.

THE BOOK OF PROVERBS

*A*S THE EVENING FALLS, DEAR LORD, and while I seek Your face in prayers, grant me the joy of good friends, the creative power of new interests, and the peace of a quiet heart. As darkness comes grant me light to judge the errors and the wisdom of the day's work. And grant me again the healing touch of sleep. Amen.

AUTHOR UNKNOWN

Prayer is and remains always a native and deepest impulse of the soul of man....Prayer is a turning of one's soul, in heroic reverence, in infinite desire and endeavor, towards the Highest, the All-Excellent, Omnipotent, Supreme.

THOMAS CARLYLE

Let our prayers,
like the ancient sacrifices,
ascend morning and evening;
let our days begin
and end with God.

WILLIAM CHANNING

*A*ND WE PRAY, give us such awareness of Your mercies, that with truly thankful hearts we may make known Your praise, not only with our lips, but in our lives, by giving up ourselves to Your service, and by walking before You in holiness and righteousness all our days; through Jesus Christ our Lord, to whom, with You and the Holy Spirit, be all honor and glory throughout the ages. Amen.

THE BOOK OF COMMON PRAYER

Expect to have hope rekindled.
Expect your prayers to be
answered in wondrous ways.
The dry seasons in life do not last.
The spring rains will come again.

SARAH BAN BREATHNACH

Prayer is the answer
to every problem there is.

OSWALD CHAMBERS

ORD, HELP ME TO BE GOOD...I fully realize that I don't have what it takes without Your help. Take my selfishness, impatience, and irritability and turn them into kindness, long-suffering, and the willingness to bear all things. Take my old emotional habits, mindsets, automatic reactions, rude assumptions, and self-protective stance, and make me patient, kind, good, faithful, gentle, and self-controlled. Take the hardness of my heart and break down the walls with Your battering ram of revelation. Give me a new heart and work in me Your love, peace, and joy. I am not able to rise above who I am at this moment. Only You can transform me.

STORMIE OMARTIAN

Prayer is the rustling of the wings of the angels who are bringing the blessing to us.

CHARLES SPURGEON

To have, each day, the thing I wish,

Lord, that seems best to me;

But not to have the thing I wish,

Lord, that seems best to Thee.

Most truly, then, Thy will is done,

When mine, O Lord, is crossed;

'Tis good to see my plans o'erthrown,

My ways in Thine all lost.

Horatius Bonar

Our prayers are answered
not when we are given
what we ask but when
we are challenged to be
what we can be.

Morris Alder

LMIGHTY AND EVERLASTING GOD, who hatest nothing that Thou hast made, and dost forgive the sins of all them that are penitent; create and make in us new and contrite hearts, that we, worthily lamenting our sins, may obtain of Thee, the God of all mercy, perfect remission and forgiveness; through Jesus Christ our Lord. Amen.

THE BOOK OF COMMON PRAYER

To pray is the greatest thing
we can do....True praying has
the largest results for good;
and poor praying, the least.

E. M. BOUNDS

ORD, I AM IN WANT, BE PLEASED TO SUPPLY ME; but, meanwhile, if thou do not, I believe it is better for me to be in need, and so I praise thee for my necessity while I ask thee to supply it. I glory in mine infirmity, even while I ask thee to overcome it. I triumph before thee in my affliction, and bless thee for it even while I ask thee to help me in it and to rescue me out of it.

CHARLES SPURGEON

We breathe our secret wish,
The importunate longing
which no man may see;
We ask it humbly,
or, more restful still,
We leave it all to Thee.

SUSAN COOLIDGE

EAR FATHER, it is my greatest desire today to know You better. I want to have a relationship with You that is distinguished by intimacy of prayer, integrity of life, and intentionality of commitment. You have searched me, and You know me. If there is any sin in me, forgive it and lead me to the truth of Your absolutes for living. Thank You for guiding all my relationships and responsibilities. Lead my steps today so that I may live out Your intentions for my life. Give me the peace of knowing and trusting You completely. In the grace of Your beloved Son. Amen.

LLOYD JOHN OGILVIE

Prayer is not the mystical experience of a few special people, but an aggressive act...an act that may be performed by anyone who will accept the challenge to learn to pray.

JACK HAYFORD

O LORD, Thou knowest what is best for us; let this or that be done, as Thou shalt please. Give what Thou wilt, and how much Thou wilt, and when Thou wilt. Deal with me as Thou thinkest good. Set me where Thou wilt, and deal with me in all things just as Thou wilt. Behold, I am Thy servant, prepared for all things: for I desire not to live unto myself, but unto Thee; and oh, that I could do it worthily and perfectly!

THOMAS À KEMPIS

When we rely upon organization,
we get what organization can do;
when we rely upon education,
we get what education can do;
when we rely upon eloquence,
we get what eloquence can do.
And so on. But when we rely upon
prayer, we get what God can do.

A. C. DIXON

FATHER, WE THANK THEE FOR THE NIGHT,

And for the pleasant morning light;

For rest and food and loving care,

And all that makes the world so fair.

Help us to do the things we should,

To be to others kind and good;

In all we do, in work or play,

To love Thee better day by day.

REBECCA WESTON
"CHILD'S MORNING HYMN"

Be joyful in hope,
patient in affliction,
faithful in prayer.

THE BOOK OF ROMANS

WE KNOW THAT HE PRAYS THAT SERVES, he praises that gives, he adores that obeys, and the life is the best music. Oh! set it to good music, we pray Thee, and help us all through to keep to each note, and may there be no false note in all the singing of our life, but all be according to that sacred score which is written out so fully in the life music of our Lord. We beseech Thee to look down upon Thy children, and cheer us. Lord, lift us up. Come, Holy Spirit, like a fresh bracing wind, and let our spirit, through Thy Spirit, rise upward toward God.

CHARLES SPURGEON

Feel often during the day the need for prayer and pray. Prayer opens the heart, till it is capable of containing God Himself. Ask and seek and your heart will be big enough to receive Him and keep Him as your own.

MOTHER THERESA

FATHER **G**OD, we come to You this day to ask for forgiveness of our sins. We repent and ask for Your mercies. We ask that You give us added strength that we might not repeat these sins against You. May our lives reflect the grace that You extend to us. Amen.

BOB AND EMILIE BARNES

Prayer is not asking.
Prayer is putting oneself
in the hands of God,
at His disposition, and
listening to His voice in
the depths of our heart.

AUTHOR UNKNOWN

Prayers are heard in heaven very much
in proportion to our faith.
Little faith gets very great mercies,
but great faith still greater.

CHARLES SPURGEON

FATHER, LET OUR FAITHFUL MIND

Rest, on Thee alone inclined;

Every anxious thought repress,

Keep our souls in perfect peace.

CHARLES WESLEY

Sweet hour of prayer, sweet hour of prayer,

Thy wings shall my petition bear

To Him, whose truth and faithfulness

Engage the waiting soul to bless;

And since He bids me seek His face,

Believe His word, and trust His grace,

I'll cast on Him my every care,

And wait for thee, sweet hour of prayer.

WILLIAM W. WALFORD
"SWEET HOUR OF PRAYER"

$\mathcal{G}$RACIOUS LORD, HAVE MERCY ON ME! Thank You for giving me the peace of knowing that when I feel lost and forsaken, You will save me with daily experiences of Your amazing grace. When I cry out to You, You will answer. Thank You for Your inexhaustible and all-sufficient grace, offered to me even before I know I need it. In the name of Jesus Christ, the grace of Your heart. Amen.

LLOYD JOHN OGILVIE

This is the business of our life.
By labor and prayer to advance
in the grace of God, till we come
to that height of perfection which,
with clean hearts, we may behold God.

ST. AUGUSTINE

Make me patient,
kind, and gentle,
Day by day;
Teach me how
to live more nearly
As I pray.

AUTHOR UNKNOWN

Paintings

Our Father in heaven,

hallowed be your name,

your kingdom come,

your will be done

on earth as it is in heaven.

Give us today our daily bread.

Forgive us our debts,

as we also have forgiven our debtors.

And lead us not into temptation,

but deliver us from the evil one.

THE BOOK OF MATTHEW